```
I0118876
```

Table of Contents

PREFACE

MESSAGE TO THE READER

Dear Reader,

Thank you for choosing this edition; it is more than just a book—you are reading a living thread of humanity's literary heritage.

We'd like to invite you to **gain immediate, unlimited digital & audiobook access** to hundreds of the most treasured literary classics ever written—along with the option to **secure deluxe paperback, hardcover & box set editions at printing cost.** Together, we can **spark a new global literary renaissance** alongside our small, independent publishing house called "The Library of Alexandria."

Thousands of years ago, the Library of Alexandria stood as a beacon of knowledge—until it was lost to history. We aim to reignite that spirit of preservation and discovery right now, in the modern age—only this time, it's accessible to all, in every language and every format.

Picture a world where every timeless classic, novel, poem, or philosophical treatise is not only available to read but also updated for today's readers—modernized, translated into any language or dialect, and ready to enjoy in any format you choose, whether that is in an eBook, audiobook, paperback, or deluxe hardcover & box set version a printing cost.

By joining our movement to **rebuild the modern Library of Alexandria**, you become part of an unprecedented mission to offer:

- **Unlimited Audiobook & eBook Access to the Greatest Classics of All Time**

  Instantly explore thousands of legendary works, from Plato and Shakespeare to Jane Austen and Leo Tolstoy. All are instantly ready to read or listen to, giving you a complete literary universe at your fingertips.

- **Paperback & Deluxe Editions at Printing Costs:**

  Purchase any title in a paperback, deluxe hardbound, or deluxe boxset edition at printing costs, shipped right to your doorstep. Curate your personal library of Alexandria with editions worthy of display—crafted to last, designed to captivate, and delivered straight to your door.

- **Modern translations for Contemporary Readers in all languages and dialects**

  Discover a vast selection of classics reimagined in clear, current language—no more struggling with outdated phrases or obscure references. Next to the original versions, we aim to offer translations in as many languages and dialects as possible.

As we continue our translation efforts and add new languages, readers everywhere can connect with these works as if they were written today. *By bridging linguistic divides, you're contributing to ensuring that these timeless stories become more meaningful, accessible, and inspiring for people across the globe.*

- **Your Personal Library of Alexandria:**

  Over the months and years, you'll curate a unique physical archive of classics—each volume a testament to your taste, curiosity, and love of knowledge. It's not just about owning books—it's about curating a cultural legacy you'll cherish and pass down for generations to come.

- **Join a Global Literary Renaissance:**

  Your support fuels an ongoing mission: allowing us to reinvest in offering deluxe print editions (including special boxsets) at their true cost, broaden the range of available formats and translations, and extend the reach of these works to new audiences worldwide. By joining today, you're not just preserving a legacy of masterpieces; *you set in motion a powerful wave of literary accessibility.*

We are more than a publisher—we're a movement, and we can't do it alone. Your support lets us scale our mission, preserving and reimagining history's greatest works for tomorrow's readers.

Become a Torchbearer of knowledge.

Thank you for picking up this book and allowing us into your literary journey. As you turn the pages, know that you're part of something larger: a global effort to keep these stories alive, share their wisdom across borders and generations, and spark a true cultural revival for the modern era.

If this resonates with you—please consider taking the next step. By visiting:
www.libraryofalexandria.com

With gratitude and a shared love of knowledge,

The Modern Library of Alexandria Team

Visit:

www.libraryofalexandria.com

Or scan the code below:

On Memory and Reminiscence

The Science of Memory and Thought

A Modern Translation

Adapted for the Contemporary Reader

Aristotle

Translated by Tim Zengerink

Introduction

Ancient Greece was a civilization famous for its great contributions to philosophy, politics, art, and science. It thrived from the 8th century BCE until the Roman Empire started to decline. Greece's city-states, especially Athens, were the heart of culture and intellectual thought. This was the time when democracy began, impressive buildings like the Parthenon were built, and famous playwrights like Sophocles and Euripides produced their works. The Greeks' curiosity about the world around them laid the foundation for Western philosophy. Thinkers like Socrates, Plato, and later Aristotle, pushed the limits of what people understood about the world.

Greek society was deeply connected to theism, which focused on a large group of gods and goddesses who were believed to control every part of life. But this system did not prevent people from exploring new ideas. In fact, it coexisted with a growing interest in finding logical explanations for nature and human

life. Intellectuals would often debate and discuss these ideas in public places like the Agora. Aristotle grew up in this dynamic environment, learning from earlier philosophers, and later challenging and expanding their ideas.

Aristotle's Life

Aristotle was born in 384 BCE in a small town called Stagira, located in northern Greece. His father, Nicomachus, was a doctor for King Amyntas of Macedon, and this allowed Aristotle to be around the Macedonian royal court from a young age. When his parents passed away, Aristotle was sent to Athens at the age of 17 to pursue his education. Athens was the center of intellectual life in Greece, and Aristotle joined Plato's Academy, which was the most respected school of the time. The Academy was a place where students discussed everything from ethics to science. Although Aristotle learned a lot from Plato, he did not always agree with him, especially when it came to metaphysics, which deals with the nature of reality.

After spending almost 20 years at the Academy, Aristotle left Athens around 347 BCE after Plato's death. He traveled around different cities in Greece, continuing to study and learn. In 343 BCE, he was

invited to the court of King Philip II of Macedon, where he became the tutor of Philip's son, Alexander, who would later become known as Alexander the Great. Aristotle taught Alexander about philosophy, ethics, politics, and science. Aristotle's influence is visible in Alexander's leadership style, which showed respect for knowledge and strategic thinking.

After teaching Alexander, Aristotle returned to Athens in 335 BCE, where he opened his own school called the Lyceum. Unlike Plato's Academy, the Lyceum focused more on recording knowledge and observing nature. Aristotle and his students performed research, studied animals, and took notes on what they observed. The Lyceum became a major center of learning, and it rivaled Plato's Academy. This is also where Aristotle wrote many of his famous works.

Later in life, after the death of Alexander in 323 BCE, the political climate in Athens became difficult for Aristotle because of his connections to the Macedonian court. Accused of disrespecting the gods, Aristotle decided to leave Athens. He fled to Chalcis, where he passed away in 322 BCE. Even though he had to leave Athens, his legacy lived on through his many writings and the influence of his school, the Lyceum.

Aristotle's Impact on Western Thought

No figure looms larger over the development of Western philosophy and science than Aristotle. A student of Plato and tutor to Alexander the Great, he unified logic, ethics, politics, rhetoric, and metaphysics into a coherent system that shaped intellectual inquiry for centuries. Although his writings reflect the best knowledge of his era, they also reveal a distinctive way of understanding the world—one that balances observation with rigorous logical analysis. Over time, this method has profoundly influenced everything from political theory to modern scientific methodology.

Aristotle approached knowledge as an interconnected whole, seeing each field of study as a vital path toward truth. While many earlier thinkers focused on abstract concepts, he emphasized direct observation of the natural world. By systematically examining and classifying what he saw, Aristotle laid the groundwork for the empirical methods now central to modern science. Although our understanding of nature has evolved, his legacy endures in today's emphasis on evidence-based research.

Logic: The Foundation of Rational Inquiry

Often hailed as the "father of formal logic," Aristotle introduced a system of reasoning that shaped intellectual discourse for over two millennia. In works like the Organon, he analyzed how valid conclusions are drawn from premises and introduced syllogisms—deductive arguments that became standard tools in philosophy, theology, and science. Even contemporary logic, despite its modern mathematical and symbolic advancements, can trace many of its core principles back to Aristotle's pioneering analyses.

Metaphysics: Exploring the Nature of Reality

Aristotle's Metaphysics offered one of the earliest comprehensive explorations of existence at its most fundamental level. There, he described the nature of "being qua being" and introduced the concepts of potentiality and actuality to explain how things change and develop. These ideas deeply influenced medieval scholastics—both Christian and Islamic—who integrated Aristotelian reasoning into their theological frameworks. Today, discussions about consciousness, identity, and free will still reference these Aristotelian notions.

Ethics and the Pursuit of the Good Life

In the Nicomachean Ethics, Aristotle proposed that the ultimate aim of human life is eudaimonia, often translated as "happiness" or "flourishing." He argued that we achieve this through virtue, developed by cultivating good habits guided by reason. His famous Doctrine of the Mean asserts that moral virtue resides between two extremes—for instance, courage lies between recklessness and cowardice. This focus on character formation has profoundly shaped the tradition known as "virtue ethics," influencing modern debates on moral education, personal development, and what it means to live well.

Politics: The Role of the Individual in the City-State

Aristotle's practical approach to ethics naturally extended into political theory. In Politics, he explored various forms of government—monarchy, aristocracy, oligarchy, democracy—and weighed their merits and pitfalls. For Aristotle, a well-ordered polis (city-state) exists not merely for survival or trade but to enable its citizens to live virtuous, fulfilling lives. His conviction that ethics

and politics are intertwined remains influential, informing contemporary discussions on citizenship, governance, and justice.

Rhetoric: The Art of Persuasion

In his treatise Rhetoric, Aristotle examined how persuasion works, detailing how arguments must appeal to ethos (credibility), pathos (emotion), and logos (logic). This clear framework for effective communication continues to guide public speakers, legal advocates, and writers. From ancient courtroom orations to modern political campaigns, Aristotelian rhetoric underpins many of the strategies people use to sway audiences and shape public opinion.

Beyond these core subjects, Aristotle made significant contributions to biology, physics, psychology, and aesthetics. In the Poetics, for example, he investigated why humans respond so powerfully to tragic drama, pioneering the concept of catharsis— the emotional release that audiences feel through art. Throughout the medieval period, thinkers like Thomas Aquinas integrated Aristotle's theories into Christian theology, while Islamic philosophers such as Avicenna and Averroes preserved, interpreted, and expanded upon his works.

Across centuries of reinterpretation and debate, Aristotle remains a living voice in contemporary thought. His insistence on systematically gathering evidence and connecting it to logical principles laid the foundation for what we now recognize as the scientific method. His inquiries into human flourishing, civic responsibility, and the nature of argument continue to spark discussion and inspire new research. From personal ethics to societal organization, Aristotle's ideas help us frame enduring questions about how best to live, learn, and understand reality.

In sum, Aristotle stands as a foundational pillar of Western thought. He bridged abstract theorizing and practical inquiry, bequeathing a vision of knowledge that values both reason and experience. From ethics and politics to science and art, his ideas have been woven into countless intellectual traditions. Even today, as we grapple with questions of morality, governance, and truth, we walk in the footsteps of an ancient thinker whose breadth of insight and depth of analysis continue to guide our pursuit of wisdom.

Final Thoughts

By preserving Aristotle's legacy, we protect the intellectual depth and rigor that defined his way

of understanding the world. His systematic way of asking questions, his classification of knowledge, and his ethical theories are still relevant today, providing a model for critical thinking across many subjects. This preservation is important not just for philosophy students but for anyone interested in the foundations of human thought and the development of ideas that shape the world we live in.

One of the difficulties in studying Aristotle's work is that his ideas and language are complex. Translating these works into our modern language is a key step in making his profound insights easier for more people to understand. By putting his ideas into today's language, more readers can engage with his thoughts, even if they don't have a background in classical studies. Making Aristotle's work accessible means adapting them to modern ways of thinking without losing their original depth. This helps bridge the gap between ancient and modern readers, making sure Aristotle's work stays relevant.

On Memory and Reminiscence

Next, we need to talk about memory and remembering—what they are, what causes them, and which part of the soul they belong to, along with the process of recollecting. People who have a good memory are not always the same people who are good at recollecting. In fact, people who are slow thinkers tend to have a better memory, while those who are quick-witted and clever are better at recollecting.

First, we need to understand what memory is about, because this is where mistakes often happen. You can't remember the future; that's more a matter of opinion or expectation. Some people even believe there is a science of expectation, like divination. You also can't remember the present; this is something we only experience through our senses. By using our senses, we don't know the future or the past, only the present. But memory is always about the past. No one would say they remember something that's happening in the moment, like seeing a white object as they look at it. And you wouldn't say you remember something you are actively thinking about, like when you are studying or contemplating something right now. In these cases, you're simply perceiving or knowing it. But when someone knows something, and they aren't actively thinking about it, that's when they remember it. For example, you remember that the angles of a triangle add up to two right angles, or that you learned something before, or you heard or saw something before. Whenever you remember, you think to yourself, "I heard this before" or "I thought of this before."

So, memory is not the same as perception or understanding, but it is something that happens to one of these after some time has passed. As mentioned earlier, there is no such thing as remembering the present. The present is for perception, and the future is for expectation, but the past is what we remember. All memory, therefore, involves time passing. Only animals that can perceive time are capable of remembering, and the organ that helps them perceive time is also the one that helps them remember.

We've already discussed the idea of "presentation" in the work *On the Soul*. Without a presentation, intellectual activity is impossible. There is a similar process in geometric demonstrations. For example, when we draw a triangle, we don't focus on its exact size, but we still draw it with a specific size. Likewise, when we use our intellect, even if we are thinking about something abstract like first principles, we still imagine it as having size or quantity, even though we aren't really thinking about its size. On the other hand, if we are thinking about something that is normally quantitative but not fixed in size, we still imagine it as having a specific size, and only later do we ignore that part. Why we can't use our intellect without also thinking about continuous things like time is another question. We understand size and movement using the same part of us that understands time (which is also the part that remembers). The presentation involved in this understanding is something that affects the "common sense" we all have. So, the way we understand things like size, movement, and time comes from the primary ability to perceive. Therefore, memory, even of intellectual things, involves some kind of presentation. This means memory belongs to the faculty of perception in a direct way, while it only belongs to the intellect indirectly.

This explains why not only humans and animals with opinions or intelligence, but also certain other animals, have memory. If memory were purely about intellect, many lower animals wouldn't have memory, and probably no mortal beings would have it. As things stand, not all animals have memory because not all can perceive time. Whenever someone remembers seeing, hearing, or learning something, they have to recognize that this happened before. And the idea of "before" and "after" is about time.

So, if we ask which part of the soul is responsible for memory, it's clear that it's the part responsible for "presentation." All things that can be presented to us through our senses are immediately objects of memory, while things that involve the intellect are remembered indirectly, only through presentation.

One might wonder how it's possible to remember something that isn't there, especially since the experience (or presentation) itself is happening in the present. This is because we have to think of the memory as something like a picture. When we perceive something, it makes an impression on our minds, like a seal stamping an image onto wax. This is why people who are very emotional or are at a certain stage in life may not form memories, just as a seal wouldn't leave an impression on running water. In some people, the surface that receives the impression may be too worn out, like an old wall, or too hard, so the impression doesn't form at all. This is why very young and very old people have trouble with memory—they are either growing too fast or decaying. Similarly, people who think too fast or too slow have bad memories. The fast ones are too soft, so the impression doesn't last, while the slow ones are too hard, so no impression is made.

But if this is how memory works, we might wonder: when someone remembers something, are they remembering the impression itself, or are they remembering the thing the impression represents? If it's the impression, then it seems we wouldn't remember anything that isn't present. But if it's the thing itself, how can we remember something that isn't there, since we are only perceiving the impression? Even if we accept that there is something like a picture or an impression inside us, why does seeing this picture count as remembering the original thing and not just the picture itself? When someone remembers, they are focusing on the impression. So how do they remember something that isn't there, like they are seeing or hearing something that's not present?

The answer is that this kind of experience actually makes sense and does happen. Think of a painting on a panel—it is both a painting and a likeness. Even though it's one thing, it can be seen in two ways: as just a painting or as a likeness of something else. In the same way, the memory we hold inside us can be seen just as it is, or it can be seen as a representation of something else. When we focus on it by itself, it's just an image or a presentation, but when we see it as related to something else, it becomes a memory of that thing. When the memory is brought into our mind, if we focus on it as it is, we just have a thought. But if we think of it as being connected to something else, like a painting of a person we've never seen before, and we think of it as being a likeness of that person, then we are having a different experience. In the case of memory, one object in the mind is simply a thought, but the other is a memory because it's seen as a likeness of something else.

This explains why sometimes, when we have a certain thought or image in our minds, we aren't sure whether it's a memory or not. We might doubt whether we actually had the experience. But then, suddenly, we might get the idea that we've seen or heard this before. This happens when we shift our view from just thinking of the image by itself to thinking of it as connected to something else.

The opposite also happens, like in the case of people who are confused, like Antipheron of Oreus and others who suffer from mental disorders. They treat their random thoughts as if they were memories of things that actually happened. This happens when someone sees something that isn't really a likeness but treats it as if it is.

Mnemonic exercises, or memory exercises, are about helping someone remember something by constantly reminding them of it. This means looking at something repeatedly as a likeness, not just as a disconnected image.

So, we have now explained what memory is: it is a state where a presentation acts like a likeness of something else. As for which part of us is responsible for memory, we've shown that it is the part of our perception that also helps us understand time.

Next, we talk about recollection, and to explain it, we need to build on what we already discussed earlier. Recollection is not the same as gaining or recovering a memory. When someone first learns something, whether it's a scientific fact or something they've seen or experienced, they don't immediately recover a memory. That's because no memory has been formed before that moment, nor do they gain one from the start. It's only when this experience or knowledge becomes embedded in the soul that memory is formed. Therefore, memory doesn't happen at the same time the experience is happening.

Further, at the moment when the sensory experience or knowledge is fully embedded, a memory is established in the person who experienced it. This may involve sensory experiences or knowledge, which can sometimes be called scientific knowledge. One may remember, in an indirect way, certain things that are known scientifically. But remembering something, in the strict sense, only happens after time has passed. We remember things that we saw or experienced in the past; the moment of the original experience and the moment of remembering it are never the same.

Also, even after time has passed and one can be said to have a memory, that doesn't necessarily mean it's recollection. It's possible to remember something without actively trying to recollect it, just as a continued result of the original experience. But when someone retrieves a piece of knowledge or a memory after having forgotten it for a while, this retrieval is recollection. Remembering doesn't always mean you're recollecting, but recollecting always involves remembering, and the memory comes after successfully recollecting.

However, the idea that recollection means bringing back something that was once in your mind but was lost needs to be looked at more closely. This might be true, but it can also be false. For example, someone might learn the same thing twice from a teacher or discover it twice on their own. So, recollection should be defined differently from these acts; it must include something additional in the person who recollects, something beyond what they had when they first learned the information.

Recollection happens because one movement in the mind naturally leads to another. When these movements follow a necessary order, whenever the first movement happens, the second one will follow. If the order isn't necessary but just common, the second movement will follow most of the time. Some movements, after just one experience, leave a deeper impression than others do after many experiences. That's why some things, which we see or experience just once, are remembered better than others that we've seen many times.

So, when we are recollecting, we go through a series of earlier movements until we finally get to the one we are trying to remember. This explains why, when we try to remember, we search through thoughts, starting either from something we're currently thinking about or from something similar, opposite, or connected to what we're trying to remember. This is how recollection works: the movements we start with either match, happen at the same time, or form part of the movements of the idea we're trying to recall. So, the part we need to remember next is smaller and easier to reach.

That's how people go about recollecting, and it's also why we can sometimes recollect without even trying. The movement needed for recollection sometimes just comes after a different movement that set the stage for it. Usually, it's only after the earlier movements are triggered that the one needed for recollection follows. We don't need to trace a long chain of events to see how recollection works; even a short series will show the same process. It's clear that the method is the same in every case: one goes through a series of ideas, without having already searched for it or remembered it beforehand. Besides the natural order of experiences, there's also a customary order, and through habit, one movement often follows another in a predictable way.

So, when someone wants to recollect something, they start with a movement that will lead to the movement they want to recall. This is why attempts at recollection work best when they begin from the right starting point. The movements of memory follow one another in the same order as the original events. That's why things arranged in a fixed order, like steps in a geometric proof, are easier to remember, while things that are badly arranged are harder to remember.

Recollecting is also different from relearning in another way: when you recollect, you can, on your own, move from the first point to the next. If you can't do this without help from the outside, then you don't remember, and of course, you can't recollect. It often happens that even when someone can't recollect right away, they eventually succeed after trying. They do this by setting off many mental movements until they finally hit on one that leads to the memory they're seeking. Remembering (which is a requirement for recollecting) involves having a movement in the mind that can trigger the desired recollection. As we've said, this happens when the movements come from within the person.

But you have to find a starting point first. This is why people sometimes use memory tricks to help them recollect. They quickly move from one thought to another, like from milk to the color white, from white to mist, and from mist to moisture, which helps them remember autumn if that's what they were trying to recollect.

In general, starting from the middle of a series of events is often a good way to help you recollect any of them. If you don't remember before reaching the middle point, you might do so once you get there, or if not, nothing will help you. For example, if you're trying to recall a series of symbols like A, B, G, D, E, Z, I, H, O, and you don't remember what you want at E, you might remember O because from E, you could go toward D or Z. But if you're not searching for D or Z, then you might remember what you're looking for when you reach G if you were looking for H or I. But if it's none of these, you could try going back to A, and this process will apply to any series where you start from the middle. The reason you sometimes recollect and sometimes don't, even from the same starting point, is because there are different paths your mind can take, like from G to I or from G to D. If your mind doesn't take the same path as before, it will tend to follow the most familiar one. That's why we recollect things more quickly when we think about them often. Repetition makes the order feel more natural, and the more often we follow this path, the more like second nature it becomes.

However, in nature, things sometimes happen by chance or against the usual pattern, and this is even more common when habit is involved because habit doesn't follow natural law as strictly. This explains why, starting from the same point, our minds sometimes take the correct path and other times take a different one. This is especially true when something distracts the mind and pulls it off course. This also explains why, when we're trying to remember a name, we might recall a similar name but still get it wrong.

So, this is how recollection works. But the most important thing is that, for recollection to happen, we must recognize the time relationship of the thing we're trying to recollect. It's a fact that we have a way of distinguishing between longer and shorter times, similar to how we tell the difference between large and small spaces. It's not like some say, that our mind stretches out to the objects, like how they think our eyes send out rays to see things. Instead, we understand them through a proportional mental movement. Our minds hold similar forms and movements to the objects and events we've experienced, so thinking of larger or smaller objects happens in the same way. Therefore, just as we have forms in our minds that are proportional to the size of things, we also have something in our minds that is proportional to the time it took to experience them. Just like when you have movements in your mind between two points, you can recreate the original event in your mind.

Why, then, does the mind recall one thing rather than another? It's because the movement in the mind matches the proportions of what we're trying to remember. If the mental movement matches the event and the time, then we remember. If we only have one of these, then we don't.

There are two types of time-related movements in memory. Sometimes, when we remember a fact, we don't have a specific sense of the time it happened, like remembering we did something two days ago. Other times, we do have a clear sense of when it happened. Even when we don't clearly remember the time, we are still genuinely remembering. People often say they remember something but don't know exactly when it happened. This happens when they can't determine the length of time that passed.

People who have a good memory aren't necessarily the same people who are quick at recollecting. Recollection is different from remembering, not only in terms of time but also in that many animals can remember, but none that we know of, except humans, can recollect. The reason is that recollection is a kind of reasoning. Someone trying to recollect something concludes that they must have seen, heard, or experienced it before, and this process is like an investigation. Investigating in this way is something only animals with the ability to reason can do.

That recollection is connected to the body is proven by the fact that, when some people try hard to recollect but fail, the effort makes them uncomfortable. This discomfort persists even after they stop trying to recollect, especially in people who are melancholic. These people are particularly affected by things they imagine. The reason recollection isn't entirely under our control is similar to why someone who throws a stone can't stop it after it's been thrown. Once you start trying to recollect something, you set a process in motion in a physical part of the body where the memory resides. Those with moisture around the part of the body that controls perception feel the most discomfort from this. Once the moisture is set in motion, it's not easily calmed until the memory is found, and the process is complete. That's why feelings like anger or fear, once triggered, don't go away immediately, even if the person tries to calm themselves down. The emotions keep pushing forward, just like how someone might struggle to stop saying a word or humming a tune that's stuck in their head.

People with large upper bodies, like dwarfs, tend to have weaker memories compared to those with smaller upper bodies. This is because the extra weight presses down on the organ of perception, and their memory movements are scattered and unable to stay on track. These movements also struggle to find a direct path when trying to recollect. Children and elderly people also have weaker memories because there is too much movement in their bodies. The elderly are breaking down, and the young are still growing. Additionally, young children are physically similar to dwarfs.

This is our theory about memory and how remembering works. It explains the part of the soul that animals use to remember and how recollection happens, its definition, and the causes behind it.

• • •

On Dreams

*Aristotle's Philosophical and
Scientific Inquiry into Dreaming*

A Modern Translation

Adapted for the Contemporary Reader

Aristotle

Translated by Tim Zengerink

Introduction

Ancient Greece was a civilization famous for its great contributions to philosophy, politics, art, and science. It thrived from the 8th century BCE until the Roman Empire started to decline. Greece's city-states, especially Athens, were the heart of culture and intellectual thought. This was the time when democracy began, impressive buildings like the Parthenon were built, and famous playwrights like Sophocles and Euripides produced their works. The Greeks' curiosity about the world around them laid the foundation for Western philosophy. Thinkers like Socrates, Plato, and later Aristotle, pushed the limits of what people understood about the world.

Greek society was deeply connected to theism, which focused on a large group of gods and goddesses who were believed to control every part of life. But this system did not prevent people from exploring new ideas. In fact, it coexisted with a growing interest in finding logical explanations for nature and human

life. Intellectuals would often debate and discuss these ideas in public places like the Agora. Aristotle grew up in this dynamic environment, learning from earlier philosophers, and later challenging and expanding their ideas.

Aristotle's Life

Aristotle was born in 384 BCE in a small town called Stagira, located in northern Greece. His father, Nicomachus, was a doctor for King Amyntas of Macedon, and this allowed Aristotle to be around the Macedonian royal court from a young age. When his parents passed away, Aristotle was sent to Athens at the age of 17 to pursue his education. Athens was the center of intellectual life in Greece, and Aristotle joined Plato's Academy, which was the most respected school of the time. The Academy was a place where students discussed everything from ethics to science. Although Aristotle learned a lot from Plato, he did not always agree with him, especially when it came to metaphysics, which deals with the nature of reality.

After spending almost 20 years at the Academy, Aristotle left Athens around 347 BCE after Plato's death. He traveled around different cities in Greece, continuing to study and learn. In 343 BCE, he was

invited to the court of King Philip II of Macedon, where he became the tutor of Philip's son, Alexander, who would later become known as Alexander the Great. Aristotle taught Alexander about philosophy, ethics, politics, and science. Aristotle's influence is visible in Alexander's leadership style, which showed respect for knowledge and strategic thinking.

After teaching Alexander, Aristotle returned to Athens in 335 BCE, where he opened his own school called the Lyceum. Unlike Plato's Academy, the Lyceum focused more on recording knowledge and observing nature. Aristotle and his students performed research, studied animals, and took notes on what they observed. The Lyceum became a major center of learning, and it rivaled Plato's Academy. This is also where Aristotle wrote many of his famous works.

Later in life, after the death of Alexander in 323 BCE, the political climate in Athens became difficult for Aristotle because of his connections to the Macedonian court. Accused of disrespecting the gods, Aristotle decided to leave Athens. He fled to Chalcis, where he passed away in 322 BCE. Even though he had to leave Athens, his legacy lived on through his many writings and the influence of his school, the Lyceum.

Aristotle's Impact on Western Thought

No figure looms larger over the development of Western philosophy and science than Aristotle. A student of Plato and tutor to Alexander the Great, he unified logic, ethics, politics, rhetoric, and metaphysics into a coherent system that shaped intellectual inquiry for centuries. Although his writings reflect the best knowledge of his era, they also reveal a distinctive way of understanding the world—one that balances observation with rigorous logical analysis. Over time, this method has profoundly influenced everything from political theory to modern scientific methodology.

Aristotle approached knowledge as an interconnected whole, seeing each field of study as a vital path toward truth. While many earlier thinkers focused on abstract concepts, he emphasized direct observation of the natural world. By systematically examining and classifying what he saw, Aristotle laid the groundwork for the empirical methods now central to modern science. Although our understanding of nature has evolved, his legacy endures in today's emphasis on evidence-based research.

Logic: The Foundation of Rational Inquiry

Often hailed as the "father of formal logic," Aristotle introduced a system of reasoning that shaped intellectual discourse for over two millennia. In works like the Organon, he analyzed how valid conclusions are drawn from premises and introduced syllogisms—deductive arguments that became standard tools in philosophy, theology, and science. Even contemporary logic, despite its modern mathematical and symbolic advancements, can trace many of its core principles back to Aristotle's pioneering analyses.

Metaphysics: Exploring the Nature of Reality

Aristotle's Metaphysics offered one of the earliest comprehensive explorations of existence at its most fundamental level. There, he described the nature of "being qua being" and introduced the concepts of potentiality and actuality to explain how things change and develop. These ideas deeply influenced medieval scholastics—both Christian and Islamic—who integrated Aristotelian reasoning into their theological frameworks. Today, discussions about consciousness, identity, and free will still reference these Aristotelian notions.

Ethics and the Pursuit of the Good Life

In the Nicomachean Ethics, Aristotle proposed that the ultimate aim of human life is eudaimonia, often translated as "happiness" or "flourishing." He argued that we achieve this through virtue, developed by cultivating good habits guided by reason. His famous Doctrine of the Mean asserts that moral virtue resides between two extremes—for instance, courage lies between recklessness and cowardice. This focus on character formation has profoundly shaped the tradition known as "virtue ethics," influencing modern debates on moral education, personal development, and what it means to live well.

Politics: The Role of the Individual in the City-State

Aristotle's practical approach to ethics naturally extended into political theory. In Politics, he explored various forms of government—monarchy, aristocracy, oligarchy, democracy—and weighed their merits and pitfalls. For Aristotle, a well-ordered polis (city-state) exists not merely for survival or trade but to enable its citizens to live virtuous, fulfilling lives. His conviction that ethics

and politics are intertwined remains influential, informing contemporary discussions on citizenship, governance, and justice.

Rhetoric: The Art of Persuasion

In his treatise Rhetoric, Aristotle examined how persuasion works, detailing how arguments must appeal to ethos (credibility), pathos (emotion), and logos (logic). This clear framework for effective communication continues to guide public speakers, legal advocates, and writers. From ancient courtroom orations to modern political campaigns, Aristotelian rhetoric underpins many of the strategies people use to sway audiences and shape public opinion.

Beyond these core subjects, Aristotle made significant contributions to biology, physics, psychology, and aesthetics. In the Poetics, for example, he investigated why humans respond so powerfully to tragic drama, pioneering the concept of catharsis—the emotional release that audiences feel through art. Throughout the medieval period, thinkers like Thomas Aquinas integrated Aristotle's theories into Christian theology, while Islamic philosophers such as Avicenna and Averroes preserved, interpreted, and expanded upon his works.

Across centuries of reinterpretation and debate, Aristotle remains a living voice in contemporary thought. His insistence on systematically gathering evidence and connecting it to logical principles laid the foundation for what we now recognize as the scientific method. His inquiries into human flourishing, civic responsibility, and the nature of argument continue to spark discussion and inspire new research. From personal ethics to societal organization, Aristotle's ideas help us frame enduring questions about how best to live, learn, and understand reality.

In sum, Aristotle stands as a foundational pillar of Western thought. He bridged abstract theorizing and practical inquiry, bequeathing a vision of knowledge that values both reason and experience. From ethics and politics to science and art, his ideas have been woven into countless intellectual traditions. Even today, as we grapple with questions of morality, governance, and truth, we walk in the footsteps of an ancient thinker whose breadth of insight and depth of analysis continue to guide our pursuit of wisdom.

Final Thoughts

By preserving Aristotle's legacy, we protect the intellectual depth and rigor that defined his way

of understanding the world. His systematic way of asking questions, his classification of knowledge, and his ethical theories are still relevant today, providing a model for critical thinking across many subjects. This preservation is important not just for philosophy students but for anyone interested in the foundations of human thought and the development of ideas that shape the world we live in.

One of the difficulties in studying Aristotle's work is that his ideas and language are complex. Translating these works into our modern language is a key step in making his profound insights easier for more people to understand. By putting his ideas into today's language, more readers can engage with his thoughts, even if they don't have a background in classical studies. Making Aristotle's work accessible means adapting them to modern ways of thinking without losing their original depth. This helps bridge the gap between ancient and modern readers, making sure Aristotle's work stays relevant.

On Dreams

Next, we need to explore the topic of dreams and first figure out which part of the soul is responsible for dreams—whether they come from the part that thinks or the part that senses, since these are the only ways we gain knowledge.

If using the eyes means seeing, using the ears means hearing, and using our senses means perceiving, and if there are things that all senses can detect, like shape, size, and motion, while other things like color, sound, and taste are specific to each sense, then it's clear that when animals close their eyes to sleep, they can't see anymore. The same applies to other senses. This shows that when we are asleep, we don't sense anything, so it can't be through sense-perception that we experience dreams.

But dreams don't come from opinion either. For example, in a dream, we might think a shape approaching us is a man or a horse, which would be forming an opinion, but we also think the figure is white or beautiful. However, we don't form opinions about things like color or beauty without using our senses. Even so, in dreams, we make such judgments. In a dream, we seem to see both the figure of the person and the fact that the person is white. Sometimes, while dreaming, we think about more than just the dream itself, just like we do when we are awake and sense something. We often reason about what we see. In the same way, while asleep, we sometimes think about things beyond the dream images in front of us. Anyone who tries to remember their dreams right after waking up would notice this. Some people dream about organizing things in their mind according to a memory rule, for example. They often find themselves doing more than just dreaming—they also work on placing the dream images into memory. So, it's clear that not every image in a dream is just a simple dream, and that the extra thinking we do is related to opinion.

At least, it's clear that the part of us responsible for illusions while awake—like when we are sick—is the same part that causes us to have illusions while we sleep. Even when people are healthy and know what's true, the sun still looks like it's only a foot wide. Whether the part of the soul responsible for creating images is the same or different from the part that senses things, illusions can't happen without actually seeing or perceiving something. Even seeing or hearing something incorrectly only happens if we are actually seeing or hearing something, even if it's not what we think it is. But in sleep, we don't see or hear or sense anything real. So, maybe it's true that we don't actually see anything in dreams, but that doesn't mean the senses aren't involved at all. It's possible that our senses are affected in some way during sleep, and that this affects the main sense organ, though not exactly in the same way it does when we are awake. Sometimes, even in dreams, our opinion tells us that what we are seeing isn't real, just like it does when we are awake. Other times, it follows the dream image without questioning it.

So, it's clear that dreaming isn't simply a matter of opinion or reasoning, but it's also not just a simple function of the senses. If it were only about the senses, we would be able to hear and see things in our dreams in the same way we do when we are awake.

Now we need to figure out how dreaming happens and what exactly it is. Let's assume something that's pretty clear: dreaming is related to sense-perception in the same way that sleep is. After all, sleep and dreaming don't involve different organs; both come from the same part.

Since we've already discussed in another work that creating mental images is related to sense-perception, and the ability to create images is the same as the ability to sense things (though thinking about images is different from simply sensing things), and since images come from the activity of the senses, and dreams seem to be images, it's clear that dreaming involves sense-perception, but in a way that's connected to creating images.

We can understand dreams better by looking at what happens during sleep. When we sense something, whether it's through seeing, hearing, or any other sense, the object of that sense leaves an impression on our senses. These impressions stay with us even after the object is gone.

This is like how a moving object, like a rock, keeps moving even after the thing that set it in motion stops touching it. The rock moves through the air because it pushed the air in front of it, and that air pushes the air in front of it, continuing the motion until the rock stops. The same thing happens when something causes a change in quality, like heat. If one part of something gets hot, it heats up the part next to it, and the heat spreads until the whole thing is warm. The same process happens in our sense organs. When we sense something, the sensory change continues in our organs even after the object we were sensing is gone.

This is easy to see when we focus on a particular sense for a long time. If we stare at something bright and then look at darkness, we won't see anything for a while because the light left an impression in our eyes. If we stare at a bright color like white or green, the next thing we look at will seem to have that color. If we look at the sun or something else bright and then close our eyes, we'll still see the image of the sun for a while, first in its own color, then in red, purple, and finally black before it disappears. The same thing happens if we watch something moving, like a fast-flowing river, and then look away. The still objects around us will seem to move because the impression of movement is still in our eyes. People's hearing gets worse after listening to loud sounds, and after smelling strong odors, our sense of smell is weaker. The same thing happens with all the other senses.

Our sense organs are sensitive to even small changes, as we can see by looking at mirrors. Mirrors deserve to be studied closely on their own, but they also show that just as the eyes are affected by what they see, they also affect what they look at. If a woman looks into a polished mirror while she's on her period, the surface of the mirror can become cloudy, with a reddish tint. It's hard to remove this stain from a new mirror, but easier from an old one. The reason this happens is that when we see something, the sense organ is affected by the object, but it also has an effect on the object, especially if the object is bright. Seeing involves brightness and color, and the eyes, like other body parts, have their own effects. Because the eyes are full of blood vessels, a woman's eyes change when she's on her period, but her husband won't notice this because his body is similar to hers. The air around the mirror and the person looking into it also changes, which causes the mirror's surface to be affected. Just like a clean garment gets dirty quickly, a clean mirror shows even small stains clearly. A shiny bronze mirror, for example, is especially sensitive to contact because the air around it acts like it's rubbing or pressing against it. That's why clean mirrors show even the smallest smudges. It's hard to clean a new mirror because the stain goes deep, but old mirrors don't hold stains as easily because the stains only affect the surface.

So, it's clear that even small changes can cause movements in the senses and that our sense organs respond quickly to them. It's also clear that the organ responsible for seeing color isn't just affected by the color but also affects it. We can see the same thing in how oil and wine are affected by the smells around them. Oil and wine take on the smells of things nearby, not just what's mixed with them, but also things that are close to them or grow near them.

To answer the question we started with, let's assume a few things that we know are true: even after the thing we were sensing is gone, the impression it left behind stays with us, and we can still sense it. Also, we are easily fooled by our senses when we're emotional, and different people are affected by different emotions. For example, a scared person might think they see an enemy, and a person in love might think they see the object of their desire, even if there's only a slight resemblance. The more emotional we are, the less it takes for us to be tricked by our senses. This is why people who have fevers sometimes think they see animals on the walls. The markings on the walls might look like animals, and this illusion gets stronger if the person's emotions are high. If the illness isn't too bad, they can still tell it's not real, but if they're very sick, they might start reacting to what they think they see. The reason this happens is that the part of us that judges what we see isn't the same as the part that presents the images to us. We can see this in how the sun looks small even though we know it's big. When we cross our fingers and touch something, it feels like we're touching two things instead of one, but we know there's only one because our sight is more reliable than touch. If we only relied on touch, we would believe there were two things. These false judgments happen because we can have perceptions even when the sense isn't directly interacting with the object. For example, people on a moving ship might think the land is moving when really, it's their eyes that are being moved by the ship.

It's clear from this that the movements caused by sensory impressions, whether they come from things outside the body or from within, happen not only when people are awake but even more strongly when they are asleep. During the day, when the senses and the mind are working together, these movements are pushed aside or hidden, like a small fire next to a larger one, or a small pain or pleasure compared to a greater one. When the bigger one fades, we notice the smaller one. But at night, when we sleep, because the senses are inactive and can't work properly, the movements are sent to the main center of sense-perception and show themselves once the activity of being awake fades away. We can think of these movements like small whirlpools in a river, which keep going, sometimes staying as they were when they started, but other times getting broken up by obstacles.

This explains why we don't dream right after eating or why young children, like infants, don't dream. The internal movement in these cases is too strong because of the heat generated by food. Just like in water, if it's stirred up too much, sometimes no reflection appears, or if it does, it looks distorted, not like the original image. But once the water calms down, the reflection becomes clear. In the same way, during sleep, the movements left over from sensory impressions are sometimes wiped out by this strong movement. Other times, the images are there, but they're confused and strange. The dreams that come at these times are unhealthy, like the dreams of people who are sick, have too much bile, or are drunk. All these conditions create a lot of disturbance and unrest in the body. In animals with blood, when the blood calms down and its pure parts are separated from the impure ones, the movements left from the senses remain clear, and the dreams are healthy. The dreamer then believes they are actually seeing something because of the movements coming from the sense of sight, or hearing something because of the movements coming from the sense of hearing, and so on for the other senses. It's because these movements come from the senses that we sometimes believe we are seeing, hearing, or feeling something, even when we're awake. For example, sometimes we mistakenly think we see something when the eye is not really being stimulated, or think one object is two because of the way our sense of touch is sending signals. Usually, our main sense organ accepts what each particular sense reports, unless another sense contradicts it.

In every case, something appears, but what appears doesn't always seem real unless the main sense organ is blocked or not working properly. Just as different people are fooled by different emotions when they are awake, the same happens in sleep. The sleeper, because of the movements in their senses during sleep, as well as the other sensory processes, is easily fooled. So, a dream, even if it's not exactly like reality, seems like a real thing. When we sleep, most of the blood moves inward toward the heart, and the sensory movements, some potential and some active, move inward with it. They are related to each other in such a way that if the blood is moved, one sensory movement will show up, and if that one disappears, another will take its place. They are like toy frogs in water, which rise to the surface one by one as the salt holding them down dissolves. The remaining sensory movements are like this: they are inside the soul, ready to be activated, but they only come out when the obstacles holding them back are removed. When they are released, they start to move in the small amount of blood that remains in the sense organs. These movements seem real, just like cloud shapes that quickly change into forms like humans or centaurs. Each movement is a leftover from a real sensory impression, and even after the real impression is gone, the memory of it remains. It's correct to say that, even though it's not really a person like Koriskos, it looks like him. When the person was actually sensing things, their main sense organ didn't call the image Koriskos, but rather, it called the real person "Koriskos." So now, in dreams, the sense organ receives this leftover impression from the sense organs and mistakes it for the real thing. The effect of sleep is so strong that this mistake goes unnoticed. In the same way, if you place a finger under your eyelid, you'll see two images of one object and might even believe there are two objects. But if you know your finger is there, you won't be fooled. The image remains the same, but you don't form the wrong opinion. This is how it works in sleep: if the sleeper realizes they're dreaming and is aware that what they're seeing is just a dream, the image still appears, but a voice inside tells them, "This looks like Koriskos, but the real Koriskos isn't here." Often, while dreaming, people have something in their mind telling them that what they're seeing is just a dream. But if the sleeper doesn't know they're dreaming, there's nothing to contradict the dream.

What I've said is true, and anyone can test it by paying attention to what they experience when they are falling asleep or waking up. Sometimes, just as they wake up, they catch the images that were in their dream and realize they were just movements lingering in the sense organs. Some young people, when it's dark, see lots of phantom shapes moving in front of them, even though their eyes are wide open, and they often cover their heads in fear.

From all this, we can conclude that a dream is a kind of image, and more specifically, one that happens during sleep. The phantom images I mentioned before aren't dreams, nor is anything else a dream if it happens when the senses are fully active. Also, not every image that appears during sleep is a dream. Some people, even while asleep, actually sense sounds, lights, tastes, and touch, though weakly and from a distance. There have been cases where people, while asleep with their eyes partly open, thought they saw the light of a lamp in their dream, and then, when they woke up, realized it was the real light of the lamp. In other cases, people faintly heard the crowing of a rooster or the barking of a dog and then recognized the real sounds once they woke up. Some people even answer questions while they are asleep. It's possible for both waking and sleeping to happen at the same time in different ways. But none of these things should be called dreams. Nor should real thoughts that occur during sleep be called dreams. A true dream is an image based on sensory impressions that happens while sleeping in the strict sense of the word.

Some people never dream in their entire lives, while others start dreaming later in life, having never dreamed before. The reason why some people don't dream seems to be similar to why infants and people who have just eaten don't dream. It makes sense that people who naturally have a lot of vapor rising inside them, which then settles back down, wouldn't have dreams because of the strong internal movement. But it's not surprising that as people get older, they start to dream. As they change with age or emotional experiences, it's inevitable that this shift from not dreaming to dreaming will happen.

• • •

On Sleep and Sleeplessness

Aristotle's Theory of Rest, Dreams, and Consciousness

A Modern Translation

Adapted for the Contemporary Reader

Aristotle

Translated by Tim Zengerink

Introduction

Ancient Greece was a civilization famous for its great contributions to philosophy, politics, art, and science. It thrived from the 8th century BCE until the Roman Empire started to decline. Greece's city-states, especially Athens, were the heart of culture and intellectual thought. This was the time when democracy began, impressive buildings like the Parthenon were built, and famous playwrights like Sophocles and Euripides produced their works. The Greeks' curiosity about the world around them laid the foundation for Western philosophy. Thinkers like Socrates, Plato, and later Aristotle, pushed the limits of what people understood about the world.

Greek society was deeply connected to theism, which focused on a large group of gods and goddesses who were believed to control every part of life. But this system did not prevent people from exploring new ideas. In fact, it coexisted with a growing interest in finding logical explanations for nature and human

life. Intellectuals would often debate and discuss these ideas in public places like the Agora. Aristotle grew up in this dynamic environment, learning from earlier philosophers, and later challenging and expanding their ideas.

Aristotle's Life

Aristotle was born in 384 BCE in a small town called Stagira, located in northern Greece. His father, Nicomachus, was a doctor for King Amyntas of Macedon, and this allowed Aristotle to be around the Macedonian royal court from a young age. When his parents passed away, Aristotle was sent to Athens at the age of 17 to pursue his education. Athens was the center of intellectual life in Greece, and Aristotle joined Plato's Academy, which was the most respected school of the time. The Academy was a place where students discussed everything from ethics to science. Although Aristotle learned a lot from Plato, he did not always agree with him, especially when it came to metaphysics, which deals with the nature of reality.

After spending almost 20 years at the Academy, Aristotle left Athens around 347 BCE after Plato's death. He traveled around different cities in Greece, continuing to study and learn. In 343 BCE, he was

invited to the court of King Philip II of Macedon, where he became the tutor of Philip's son, Alexander, who would later become known as Alexander the Great. Aristotle taught Alexander about philosophy, ethics, politics, and science. Aristotle's influence is visible in Alexander's leadership style, which showed respect for knowledge and strategic thinking.

After teaching Alexander, Aristotle returned to Athens in 335 BCE, where he opened his own school called the Lyceum. Unlike Plato's Academy, the Lyceum focused more on recording knowledge and observing nature. Aristotle and his students performed research, studied animals, and took notes on what they observed. The Lyceum became a major center of learning, and it rivaled Plato's Academy. This is also where Aristotle wrote many of his famous works.

Later in life, after the death of Alexander in 323 BCE, the political climate in Athens became difficult for Aristotle because of his connections to the Macedonian court. Accused of disrespecting the gods, Aristotle decided to leave Athens. He fled to Chalcis, where he passed away in 322 BCE. Even though he had to leave Athens, his legacy lived on through his many writings and the influence of his school, the Lyceum.

Aristotle's Impact on Western Thought

No figure looms larger over the development of Western philosophy and science than Aristotle. A student of Plato and tutor to Alexander the Great, he unified logic, ethics, politics, rhetoric, and metaphysics into a coherent system that shaped intellectual inquiry for centuries. Although his writings reflect the best knowledge of his era, they also reveal a distinctive way of understanding the world—one that balances observation with rigorous logical analysis. Over time, this method has profoundly influenced everything from political theory to modern scientific methodology.

Aristotle approached knowledge as an interconnected whole, seeing each field of study as a vital path toward truth. While many earlier thinkers focused on abstract concepts, he emphasized direct observation of the natural world. By systematically examining and classifying what he saw, Aristotle laid the groundwork for the empirical methods now central to modern science. Although our understanding of nature has evolved, his legacy endures in today's emphasis on evidence-based research.

Logic: The Foundation of Rational Inquiry

Often hailed as the "father of formal logic," Aristotle introduced a system of reasoning that shaped intellectual discourse for over two millennia. In works like the Organon, he analyzed how valid conclusions are drawn from premises and introduced syllogisms—deductive arguments that became standard tools in philosophy, theology, and science. Even contemporary logic, despite its modern mathematical and symbolic advancements, can trace many of its core principles back to Aristotle's pioneering analyses.

Metaphysics: Exploring the Nature of Reality

Aristotle's Metaphysics offered one of the earliest comprehensive explorations of existence at its most fundamental level. There, he described the nature of "being qua being" and introduced the concepts of potentiality and actuality to explain how things change and develop. These ideas deeply influenced medieval scholastics—both Christian and Islamic—who integrated Aristotelian reasoning into their theological frameworks. Today, discussions about consciousness, identity, and free will still reference these Aristotelian notions.

Ethics and the Pursuit of the Good Life

In the Nicomachean Ethics, Aristotle proposed that the ultimate aim of human life is eudaimonia, often translated as "happiness" or "flourishing." He argued that we achieve this through virtue, developed by cultivating good habits guided by reason. His famous Doctrine of the Mean asserts that moral virtue resides between two extremes—for instance, courage lies between recklessness and cowardice. This focus on character formation has profoundly shaped the tradition known as "virtue ethics," influencing modern debates on moral education, personal development, and what it means to live well.

Politics: The Role of the Individual in the City-State

Aristotle's practical approach to ethics naturally extended into political theory. In Politics, he explored various forms of government—monarchy, aristocracy, oligarchy, democracy—and weighed their merits and pitfalls. For Aristotle, a well-ordered polis (city-state) exists not merely for survival or trade but to enable its citizens to live virtuous, fulfilling lives. His conviction that ethics

and politics are intertwined remains influential, informing contemporary discussions on citizenship, governance, and justice.

Rhetoric: The Art of Persuasion

In his treatise Rhetoric, Aristotle examined how persuasion works, detailing how arguments must appeal to ethos (credibility), pathos (emotion), and logos (logic). This clear framework for effective communication continues to guide public speakers, legal advocates, and writers. From ancient courtroom orations to modern political campaigns, Aristotelian rhetoric underpins many of the strategies people use to sway audiences and shape public opinion.

Beyond these core subjects, Aristotle made significant contributions to biology, physics, psychology, and aesthetics. In the Poetics, for example, he investigated why humans respond so powerfully to tragic drama, pioneering the concept of catharsis— the emotional release that audiences feel through art. Throughout the medieval period, thinkers like Thomas Aquinas integrated Aristotle's theories into Christian theology, while Islamic philosophers such as Avicenna and Averroes preserved, interpreted, and expanded upon his works.

Across centuries of reinterpretation and debate, Aristotle remains a living voice in contemporary thought. His insistence on systematically gathering evidence and connecting it to logical principles laid the foundation for what we now recognize as the scientific method. His inquiries into human flourishing, civic responsibility, and the nature of argument continue to spark discussion and inspire new research. From personal ethics to societal organization, Aristotle's ideas help us frame enduring questions about how best to live, learn, and understand reality.

In sum, Aristotle stands as a foundational pillar of Western thought. He bridged abstract theorizing and practical inquiry, bequeathing a vision of knowledge that values both reason and experience. From ethics and politics to science and art, his ideas have been woven into countless intellectual traditions. Even today, as we grapple with questions of morality, governance, and truth, we walk in the footsteps of an ancient thinker whose breadth of insight and depth of analysis continue to guide our pursuit of wisdom.

Final Thoughts

By preserving Aristotle's legacy, we protect the intellectual depth and rigor that defined his way

of understanding the world. His systematic way of asking questions, his classification of knowledge, and his ethical theories are still relevant today, providing a model for critical thinking across many subjects. This preservation is important not just for philosophy students but for anyone interested in the foundations of human thought and the development of ideas that shape the world we live in.

One of the difficulties in studying Aristotle's work is that his ideas and language are complex. Translating these works into our modern language is a key step in making his profound insights easier for more people to understand. By putting his ideas into today's language, more readers can engage with his thoughts, even if they don't have a background in classical studies. Making Aristotle's work accessible means adapting them to modern ways of thinking without losing their original depth. This helps bridge the gap between ancient and modern readers, making sure Aristotle's work stays relevant.

On Sleep and Sleeplessness

When it comes to sleep and waking, we need to look at what they are: whether they belong to the soul, the body, or both; and if it's both, then what part of the soul or body they involve. We also need to find out why animals have sleep and waking, and whether all animals experience both, or if some only sleep, others only wake, or if some do neither or both.

Additionally, we need to ask what a dream is and why people sometimes dream and sometimes don't. Or maybe people always dream but don't always remember their dreams. If that's the case, we need to explain why that happens.

Another question is whether it's possible to predict the future in dreams, and if it is possible, how does it work? Also, if it's possible, does it only apply to things people will do, or also to things caused by nature, chance, or higher powers?

First, it's clear that waking and sleeping involve the same part of an animal because they are opposites, and sleep is just the absence of waking. We know that opposites, in nature and everything else, happen to the same subject. For example, health and sickness, beauty and ugliness, strength and weakness, sight and blindness, hearing and deafness—all of these happen to the same being. We can understand this better by considering how we know when someone is awake or asleep. We assume that someone who is sensing something is awake, and everyone who is awake either notices something happening outside them or feels something within themselves. So, if waking means using your senses, then it makes sense that the same organ that lets animals sense things is also what allows them to wake up or sleep.

But since sensing things isn't something that only the soul or body can do, and since sensing is a process where the soul works through the body, we can say that sensing isn't just something that happens to the soul. A body without a soul can't sense things either. So, sleep and waking don't belong to pure intelligence or lifeless bodies.

Now, we've already divided the parts of the soul before. The part that takes in nutrition can exist by itself in all living things, but none of the other parts can exist without it. This shows that sleep and waking don't happen in living things that only grow and decay, like plants. Plants don't have the ability to sense things, even if that ability can exist separately from other things. In its potential and relationships, it can be separate.

It's also clear that no animal is always awake or always asleep; both of these happen alternately in the same animals. If an animal doesn't have the ability to sense things, it can't sleep or wake up, since both sleep and waking are based on the activity of the main sense organ. It's also impossible for an animal to always be asleep or always awake because every organ that has a natural function loses its strength if it works longer than it's supposed to. For example, eyes stop working after seeing for too long, and the same happens with hands and any other part that has a job to do. If sense perception is the job of a special organ, and if this organ keeps working past its limit, it will lose its power and stop working. So, if being awake is when sense perception is working, and if some opposites can't exist at the same time while others can, then since waking and sleeping are opposites, one of them must always be present in an animal. It follows that sleep is necessary. Finally, if sleep is a state of powerlessness caused by too much waking, and if too much waking can sometimes be unhealthy, then powerlessness or loss of activity can also be healthy or unhealthy. This means that any creature that wakes up must also be able to sleep because it can't keep using its powers forever.

In the same way, no animal can always be asleep. Sleep is something that happens to the sense organ; it ties up or stops it from working. So, every creature that sleeps must have the ability to sense things. Only something that can sense things can sleep, but you can't use this ability while you're asleep. That means that everything that sleeps must also be able to wake up. We can clearly see that most animals sleep, whether they live in water, air, or on land. Fish, mollusks, and all other creatures with eyes have been observed sleeping. Creatures with hard eyes and insects show signs of sleeping, but their sleep is so short that it's hard to tell if they're really sleeping or not. On the other hand, we don't have clear evidence that shellfish sleep, but if the reasoning we've followed is convincing, we can agree that they do.

So, based on these points, we can conclude that all animals sleep. We define animals by their ability to sense things, and sleep is a kind of pause or break in sense perception, while waking up is the release or loosening of this break. Plants don't have these experiences because without sense perception, there is no sleeping or waking. But creatures that have sense perception also feel pain and pleasure, and those that feel these things also have desire. Plants don't experience any of these things. A sign of this is that the part of the body responsible for nutrition works better when the animal is asleep than when it's awake. Nutrition and growth happen more easily during sleep, which means that animals don't need sense perception to help with these processes.

Now, we need to figure out what causes sleep and waking, and which sense or senses are involved in these experiences. Some animals have all the senses, while others don't have them all. For example, some animals don't have sight, but all animals have touch and taste, except for those that are underdeveloped, which we've talked about in another work on the soul. Since an animal can't use any of its senses while asleep, sleep must involve all the senses at once. If sleep only affected one sense and not the others, then the animal could still sense things while sleeping, which is impossible.

Each sense has something unique, but they also share something in common. For example, seeing belongs to sight, hearing belongs to hearing, and so on. But all senses share a common power that lets us know when we are seeing or hearing. For sure, we don't use sight alone to know that we are seeing, and we don't use just taste or sight to understand that sweet things are different from white things. This understanding comes from a common ability that connects all the senses. This common ability is linked most closely to touch, because touch can exist without the other senses, but none of the other senses can exist without touch, as we've discussed before in our studies of the soul. Therefore, sleep and waking must involve this common and controlling sense organ. That's why sleep and waking happen in all animals, because all animals share the sense of touch.

If sleep were caused by something happening to each of the senses individually, it would be strange that all the senses, which don't always work at the same time, would stop working at the same time. You would expect the opposite, that they wouldn't all stop working together. But according to the explanation I've just given, everything makes sense. When the organ that controls all the senses, and to which all the others are connected, is affected, then it makes sense that all the others are affected at the same time. But if just one of the connected senses stops working, it doesn't necessarily mean the controlling organ will stop working too.

It's clear from many examples that sleep doesn't just mean the special senses aren't working, or that we aren't using them. That's what happens when someone faints. A faint is when the senses stop working, and other situations of unconsciousness are similar. People who have pressure on their neck blood vessels lose feeling and become unconscious. But sleep happens when this inability to use the senses doesn't come from an accident or outside cause, but when it comes from the main organ responsible for perceiving things. When this organ loses power, all the other senses also lose power. But when one of the special senses loses power, the main organ doesn't necessarily lose power too.

Next, we need to explain the cause and nature of this experience. There are different types of causes (final, efficient, material, and formal). First, we say that Nature works toward an end, and that end is good. Every creature that can move but can't move continuously needs rest. Rest is good for it. Based on experience, people compare sleep to rest, which makes sense because sleep is rest from the effort of using the senses. Sleep helps keep animals alive. But being awake is the best state for an animal because using the senses or thinking is the highest goal for any being with those abilities. These abilities are the best, and the highest goal is what's best. This means sleep is necessary for every animal. By "necessary," I mean that if an animal is going to exist and have its nature, it must have certain abilities. And if it has these abilities, it must have others as well as a condition for having the first ones.

The next thing we need to talk about is the kind of movement or activity happening inside the body that causes sleep and waking in animals. The causes of this in all animals must be the same or similar to those in animals with blood. The causes in animals with blood are the same as those in humans, so we need to study this based on examples from humans and other animals with blood. We've already decided in another work that sense perception in animals comes from the same part of the body that causes movement. This part is one of three specific areas, and it's located between the head and the stomach. In animals with blood, this part is the heart, because all animals with blood have a heart. From the heart comes both movement and control of sense perception. It's clear that movement, like breathing and cooling, starts there. Nature has designed both breathing animals and those that cool themselves with moisture to conserve the heat in this part of the body. We'll talk more about cooling later. In bloodless animals and insects, which don't breathe, the "natural spirit" puffs up and shrinks back down in the part of their body that's like the heart in animals with blood. This is easy to see in insects with undivided wings, like wasps and bees, and also in flies and other similar creatures. To move or do anything requires strength, and holding one's breath creates strength in animals that breathe. In those that don't breathe, the strength comes from holding in the natural spirit. That's why insects with undivided wings make a humming sound when they move. This sound is caused by the natural spirit rubbing against the diaphragm. Movement in any animal involves some kind of sense perception, whether it's internal or external, and it happens in the main sense organ. Since sleep and waking are experiences of this organ, the place where sleep and waking start is clear—it's where movement and sense perception begin, which is the heart.

Some people move in their sleep and do many things just like they would when awake, but they don't do this without some kind of dream or sensory experience. A dream is like a sense impression in a way, but we will talk about dreams later. Why is it that people remember their dreams when they wake up, but don't remember the things they did while asleep? We've already explained this in the book "Of Problems."

The next thing we need to consider is: What are the processes that cause waking and sleeping, and where do they come from? Since animals need to sense things in order to take in food and grow, and since in animals with blood, food turns into blood, or in animals without blood, it turns into something like blood, we must look at the veins, which hold the blood. The heart is where these veins begin, as shown by anatomy. So, when food enters the parts of the body made to receive it, the evaporation from the food enters the veins, changes, and turns into blood, which then moves toward the heart. We talked about this when we discussed nutrition, but now we need to repeat it so we can understand the beginning of this process and figure out what happens to the main organ of sense-perception that causes waking and sleep. As we've seen, sleep isn't just any lack of sensing. After all, unconsciousness, certain kinds of choking, and fainting also cause a lack of sensing. It's also a fact that some people in deep trances still have an active imagination. This creates a problem because, if someone could faint and then fall asleep while fainting, we might think the image they see in their mind is a dream. People in deep trances, who were thought to be dead, often say things while in that state. However, all of these cases should be considered as something other than sleeping or dreaming.

As we said earlier, sleep doesn't happen just because someone can't sense things; it happens because of the evaporation caused by digesting food. This evaporated matter moves to a certain point, then comes back, and changes direction, like a tide flowing through a narrow strait. In every animal, heat naturally moves upward, but once it reaches the upper parts of the body and cools, it turns back and moves downward in a mass. This is why people get sleepy after meals. The matter that moves up, both liquid and solid, is heavy in large amounts after eating. When this matter stops moving, it makes a person feel heavy and causes them to nod off. But when it moves downward and pushes the heat down, sleep comes on, and the person falls asleep. This is confirmed by the things that cause sleep. Whether it's something you drink or eat—like poppy, mandrake, wine, or darnel—all of these cause a heaviness in the head. People who are sleepy and nodding off seem to be weighed down because they can't lift their head or open their eyes. Sleep is especially common after meals because the evaporation from the food is plentiful then. Sleep can also follow certain kinds of tiredness because fatigue weakens the body, and the dissolved matter works like undigested food. Some illnesses have the same effect, especially those caused by moist and hot fluids, like fevers or lethargy. Young children also sleep a lot because all their food is carried upward. You can see this in how their upper bodies grow bigger than their lower bodies when they're babies, since growth happens more in the upper parts. This is also why children are prone to seizures, because sleep is similar to epilepsy and can be considered a type of seizure. That's why many people have their first seizure while sleeping, and their future seizures happen during sleep, not while they're awake. When the heated evaporation moves upward and then comes down again, it stretches the veins and squeezes the passage that allows breathing. This explains why wine isn't good for babies or their nurses (it doesn't matter if the baby drinks it or the nurse), and they should only drink it diluted with water and in small amounts. Wine has a lot of heat, and dark wine even more so than other kinds. The upper parts of babies are so filled with food that they don't even lift their heads in the first five months after birth. It's similar to people who are very drunk, where a lot of moisture rises in their bodies. It's also reasonable to think that this is why embryos remain still in the womb early on. As a general rule, people with small veins, dwarfs, and those with large heads tend to sleep a lot. For people with small veins, it's hard for moisture to flow through them. For dwarfs and those with large heads, the evaporation moves upward too quickly. On the other hand, people with large veins don't sleep as much because the moisture flows easily through their veins, unless something else affects them and blocks the flow. People with a lot of dark bile also don't sleep much because their internal organs are cooled, and the amount of evaporation isn't very large. That's why they tend to eat a lot but stay thin, because their bodies don't seem to get much benefit from the food they eat. The dark bile is naturally cold, and it cools the digestive system and other parts of the body where it is present.

So, from everything we've said, it's clear that sleep is a kind of gathering or pulling back of heat into the body's center, caused by the reasons mentioned earlier. That's why people who are about to fall asleep often move around restlessly. But as the heat in the upper and outer parts of the body starts to fade, they cool down, and that cooling makes their eyelids droop. During sleep, the outer and upper parts of the body are cool, but the inner and lower parts, like the feet and the inside of the body, are warm.

But we might wonder why sleep comes on so strongly after meals, even though food and drinks like wine are warm, and sleep is caused by cooling. How can sleep be a cooling process if the things that cause it are warm? The answer might be that just as the stomach is warm when it's empty and gets cooler when filled with food, the same happens in the head when the evaporation rises there. Or maybe it's like how people feel a cold shiver when hot water is poured on them. When the warm evaporation rises, the cold rushes to meet it and cools it down, forcing the heat to retreat. Also, when a lot of food is eaten, the heat that carries the evaporation upward is like a fire that cools when more logs are added until the food is digested.

As we mentioned earlier, sleep happens when the matter that is carried upward by the heat moves into the veins and goes toward the head. But when too much of this matter rises and can't keep going upward, it pushes the heat back down and flows downward. That's why people tend to fall down into sleep when the heat that helps keep them standing (since humans are the only naturally upright animals) is pushed back. When this happens, they lose consciousness and then experience dreams.

Or maybe the answers we've given don't fully explain the cooling process. Instead, the brain, or the part of the body that acts like a brain in creatures without one, may be the main cause. The brain is the coolest part of the body. Just as the sun turns moisture into vapor, and that vapor cools as it rises into the upper atmosphere and turns back into water, the same thing happens with the evaporation from food. When the evaporation is carried upward by the heat to the brain, it cools and turns into phlegm, which explains why mucus often comes from the head. The healthy evaporation, which is good for the body, cools the heat when it returns downward. The narrowness of the veins around the brain helps keep the brain cool and stops too much evaporation from reaching it. This explains how cooling happens, even though the evaporation is very hot.

A person wakes up when digestion is done, and the heat that was gathered together in one place spreads out again. At the same time, the thicker, heavier blood is separated from the finer, purer blood. The purest blood is in the head, while the thickest, most impure blood is in the lower parts of the body. The source of all blood is the heart, as we've said here and elsewhere. The central chamber of the heart connects to two other chambers. Each of these chambers is connected to one of the two main blood vessels: the "great" vessel and the "aorta." The separation of the blood happens in the central chamber. However, going into more detail about this belongs in a different discussion. After food has been digested and the pure blood has gone to the upper parts of the body while the thick blood goes to the lower parts, animals wake up, free from the heaviness caused by eating. We've now explained what causes sleep: it's the pulling back of the body's matter, moved by heat, toward the main sense organ. We've also shown what sleep is, as it shuts down the main sense organ and makes it unable to function. Sleep happens out of necessity because it's impossible for an animal to survive without the things that make it an animal, and rest is needed to keep animals alive.

The End

Thank you for Reading

Dear Reader,

We hope this timeless classic has sparked your imagination and enriched your literary journey. Now that you've turned the final page, we want to share a vision for the future of reading—one where every classic you've ever wanted to explore is at your fingertips, in a format that best suits your life.

We'd like to invite you to **gain immediate, unlimited digital & audiobook access** to hundreds of the most treasured literary classics ever written—along with the option to **secure deluxe paperback, hardcover & box set editions at printing cost**. Together, we can **spark a new global literary renaissance** alongside our small, independent publishing house called "The Library of Alexandria."

Thousands of years ago, the Library of Alexandria stood as a beacon of knowledge—until it was lost to history. We aim to reignite that spirit of preservation and discovery right now, in the modern age—only this time, it's accessible to all, in every language and every format.

Picture a world where every timeless classic, novel, poem, or philosophical treatise is not only available to read but also updated for today's readers—modernized, translated into any language or dialect, and ready to enjoy in any format you choose, whether that is in an eBook, audiobook, paperback, or deluxe hardcover & box set version a printing cost.

By joining our movement to **rebuild the modern Library of Alexandria**, you become part of an unprecedented mission to offer:

- **Unlimited Audiobook & eBook Access to the Greatest Classics of All Time**

  Instantly explore thousands of legendary works, from Plato and Shakespeare to Jane Austen and Leo Tolstoy. All are instantly ready to read or listen to, giving you a complete literary universe at your fingertips.

- **Paperback & Deluxe Editions at Printing Costs:**

  Purchase any title in a paperback, deluxe hardbound, or deluxe boxset edition at printing costs, shipped right to your doorstep. Curate your personal library of Alexandria with editions worthy of display—crafted to last, designed to captivate, and delivered straight to your door.

- **Modern translations for Contemporary Readers in all languages and dialects**

Discover a vast selection of classics reimagined in clear, current language—no more struggling with outdated phrases or obscure references. Next to the original versions, we aim to offer translations in as many languages and dialects as possible.

As we continue our translation efforts and add new languages, readers everywhere can connect with these works as if they were written today. *By bridging linguistic divides, you're contributing to ensuring that these timeless stories become more meaningful, accessible, and inspiring for people across the globe.*

- **Your Personal Library of Alexandria:**

Over the months and years, you'll curate a unique physical archive of classics—each volume a testament to your taste, curiosity, and love of knowledge. It's not just about owning books—it's about curating a cultural legacy you'll cherish and pass down for generations to come.

- **Join a Global Literary Renaissance:**

Your support fuels an ongoing mission: allowing us to reinvest in offering deluxe print editions (including special boxsets) at their true cost, broaden the range of available formats and translations, and extend the reach of these works to new audiences worldwide.

By joining today, you're not just preserving a legacy of masterpieces; *you set in motion a powerful wave of literary accessibility.*

We are more than a publisher—we're a movement, and we can't do it alone. Your support lets us scale our mission, preserving and reimagining history's greatest works for tomorrow's readers.

Become a Torchbearer of knowledge.

Thank you for picking up this book and allowing us into your literary journey. As you turn the pages, know that you're part of something larger: a global effort to keep these stories alive, share their wisdom across borders and generations, and spark a true cultural revival for the modern era.

If this resonates with you—please consider taking the next step. By visiting:
www.libraryofalexandria.com

With gratitude and a shared love of knowledge,

The Modern Library of Alexandria Team

Visit:

www.libraryofalexandria.com

Or scan the code below:

www.ingramcontent.com/pod-product-compliance
Lightning Source LLC
Chambersburg PA
CBHW010729270326
41930CB00018B/3419